Once Upon A Carpet

Kathleen Ryniker Bashian, Ph.D.

Never overlook what is underfoot

All rights reserved.
Printed in the United States of America.
No part of this publication may be used or reproduced in any manner whatsoever without written permission from the author, e-mail: culcon@mindspring.com
Copyright ©1999 Kathleen Ryniker Bashian, McLean, Virginia]

Library of Congress Catalog Number: 99-90654

ISBN I 0-9672698-0-6 hardcover
ISBN I 0-9672698-1-4 paperback

Pubished by
CULTURAL CONNECTIONS™

PRESIDENT, PUBLISHER
Kathleen Ryniker Bashian, Ph.D.

EDITOR
Andrew D. Schlessinger

DESIGNER
Teresa Crawford

ILLUSTRATOR
Mark Bashian

COVER PHOTOGRAPHY
Brenda Schrier

PRINTER
ProGraphics, Buffalo, New York

1. *Kashan* carpet.

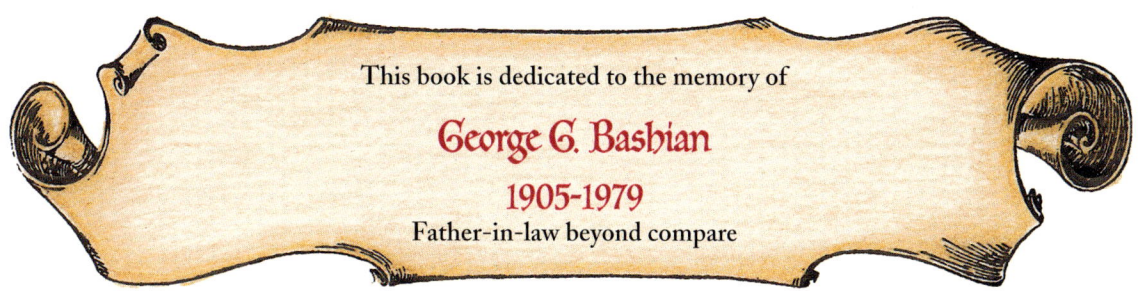

Acknowledgments

    I am deeply grateful to many oriental rug professionals who generously shared their insights, experience, and love of the carpet. Thank you, in particular, to George G. Bashian, Jr. and Behrooz Hakimian, my principal mentors and enthusiastic supporters. I appreciate as well the assistance of Roy Ryniker, Nadir Pirniakan, and Lucille Laufer.

    Peter McCarthy, Maggie Bedrosian, Miriam Keeler, and Maika Fowler each provided direction in what they know best. My staff became family and their professional signature is boldly upon this book. Heartfelt thanks to Teresa Crawford, Andy Schlessinger, Teresa Hartnett, Elizabeth Kerr, and Jim Corrin.

    My given family has lived this book with me. Thank you, my children: Mark, Kate, and George. Finally, and most especially, to my beloved husband Ron who told me I should and showed me I could accomplish this project. Each individual has made a unique and valuable contribution to bring this text to life. I am humbled by the generosity of each effort and overjoyed with the results.

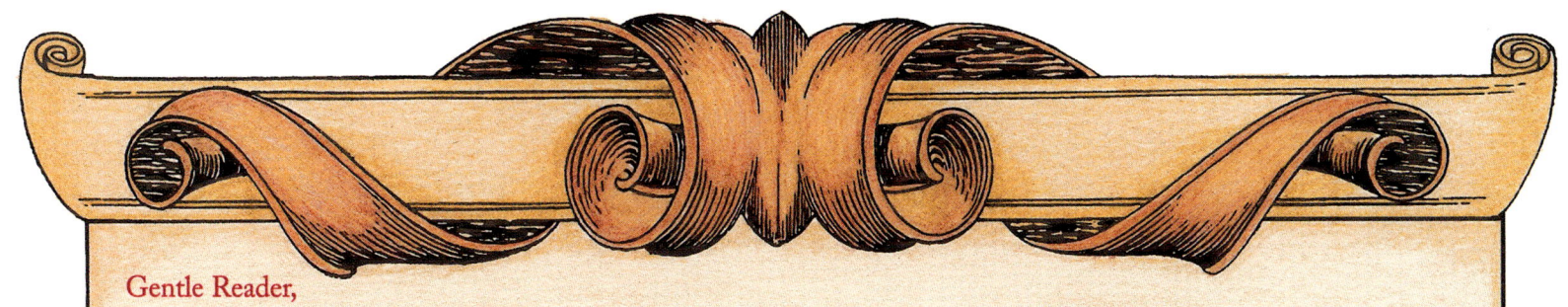

Gentle Reader,

Come join me in a celebration of oriental rugs! My welcome extends to the committed collector, experienced connoisseur, and enthusiastic *ruggie* who will each find new visions and novel, aesthetic insights into this cherished product. Curious newcomers are also invited to discover a newfound appreciation for the drama, mystery, and beauty of oriental rugs.

In these pages, cool technical facts about wool, dyes, workmanship, and rug design are joined with heartwarming stories of once-upon-a-time happenings where oriental rugs play a part in the lives of real people.

Once Upon a Carpet portrays oriental rugs in places people occupy: diplomatic, privileged, domestic, sacred, exotic, and unexpected spaces. You will find photographs, reproductions of masterwork paintings, illustrations, historical anecdotes, and personal testimonies of individuals who have bonded with rugs in their lives. I suggest particular musical compositions 𝄞 for listening pleasure, allowing you to enter more fully into the space each chapter describes.

Art begets art, and it is my intention that this book about woven works of art will engender in you the desire to creatively engage with oriental rugs. If you possess an older rug, perhaps you will begin to nostalgically reflect upon an imagined history of the creator, or previous owner, of your woven treasure. If you own a new rug, perhaps you will discover the origin and history of your carpet design even as you weave your own personal stories into it.

My hope is that you will never again overlook what is often underfoot, in your homes, museums, historical places, or sacred spaces. Let a rug touch your life to become a part of the fabric of your existence providing yet untold charm, mystery, and beauty.

Kathleen Ryniker Bashian
Cultural Connections™
McLean, Virginia
1999

Contents

I	**If These Rugs Could Talk!** Carpets in Diplomatic Space	8
II	**Roll Out The Red Carpet!** Carpets in Privileged Space	20
III	**From Cradle To Grave!** Carpets in Domestic Space	34
IV	**This Is Holy Ground!** Carpets in Sacred Space	48
V	**Oriental Mystique!** Carpets in Exotic Space	60
VI	**CarpeT Diem!** Carpets in Unexpected Space	74
	EPILOGUE	89
	ENDNOTES	90
	BIBLIOGRAPHY	93
	PICTURE CREDITS	94
	BIOGRAPHY	95

2. *Mahal* carpet.

I If These Rugs Could Talk!
Carpets in Diplomatic Space

Look into the Mahal carpet. Here is a diplomatic rug where subtlety and protocol work to reconcile differences into an agreeable whole. The carpet displays a rich variety of floral and palmette designs. Note the subtle hues, variegated colors all harmoniously contained within firm, ordered borders. This rug achieves in its woven balance the kind of reconciliation to which diplomatic negotiation aspires.

Musical Suggestion: *Islamey*, by Mili Balakirev

We enter into diplomatic space. Through stately doors, we pass into the place of tactful negotiation and consensual treaties. A diplomat in Shakespeare's time was a *carpet knight*, one who earned a title through a war of wit and words. With blunted sword, "the unhatched rapier," an envoy is left with only the pen as the weapon of choice within the carpeted space of diplomacy. How well the Bard knew the power of the pen is often mightier than the sword!

In this photo pose, on canvas, we see many carpet knights gathered at Somerset House in 1604 to negotiate the historic treaty of peace and trade between England and Spain. Here are all the elements of the paradoxical personality of oriental carpets. On the one hand, carpets lend distinction, consequence, and importance to a setting. On the other, the carpets' rich colors, lustrous sheen, and pleasing design mediate and assuage. In the painting, the English and Spanish diplomats are stiffly separated in their differences, yet the carpeted table serves to draw them together. How fitting that the tools of agreement—the parchment and quill pen with ink—rest on its surface. Centuries later we can still feel the warming effect drawing adversaries together at this table.

There is something about a rug upon a table that promotes bonding. Rugs create shared space, softening and relaxing the emotional atmosphere of almost any scene. The practice of placing carpets on tables, popular even into the early eighteenth century, tells us something of their value both as aesthetic and atmospheric conditioners. Had this practice endured, allowing carpets to hold their place on the table, think how they might figure into modern day negotiations.

The Somerset House Conference was a momentous diplomatic event between two legendary rivals. Like the carpet in the painting, the treaty required careful design and inspired craftsmanship. However, even this exquisite carpet could not guarantee lasting peace. Notice the two courtiers in the center of the portrait intently glaring at one another across the table. Was the artist prefiguring contemporary suspicions? History's footnote confirms these reservations, for rivalry between England and Spain continued long after this Somerset treaty.

Carpets In Diplomatic Space

3. The *Somerset House Conference*, Unknown master, 1604.

"He is knight, dubbed with unhatched rapier and on carpet consideration"—Shakespeare, *Twelfth Night* 3.4.235.

This photograph was taken at the historic Yalta Conference when Churchill, Roosevelt, and Stalin met together in the Crimea in 1945. The meeting took place at Livadia Palace, a fifty-room summer residence of the former Tsar Nicholas II, last emperor of Russia. Winston Churchill expressed the importance of this gathering in an opening toast, saying, "The whole world will have its eyes on this conference. If it is successful, we will have peace for a hundred years."

Was Yalta successful? Historians have long debated the political and diplomatic implications of the agreements. However, at the end of the century, we have witnessed the reunification of Germany, the institution of democracy in eastern Europe, and the stability of the United Nations. The hopes of Yalta were more than just a vision.

Study the careful arrangement in the setting of this official Yalta photograph. The Allied leaders are seated in armchairs with diplomatic advisers standing at their backs. Stone pillars, ancient symbols of strength and fortitude, appear in the distance. It is not by chance that *Sultanabad* rugs lie in this open courtyard scene. The carpets underfoot literally ground the Big Three, projecting the image of authority, strength, and unity, what the Allies hoped for at this historic moment.

Roosevelt died two months after this photograph; the alliance did not survive the year. There is an irony implicit in the photo, one of the most famous of the twentieth century. Grim fatigue on the faces of the principals offers little hope, yet the plush, velvet texture of the *Sultanabads* revives and refreshes. Where the human spirit is weary, the carpet projects life and light, the true hope of Yalta. Thankfully, it is the spirit of the carpet that ultimately prevailed.

Carpets In Diplomatic Space

4. Yalta Conference February, 1945.
Seated from left to right: Winston Churchill, Franklin D. Roosevelt and Josef Stalin. Standing immediately behind, from left: Foreign Minister Anthony Eden, Secretary of State Edward Stettinius, British Undersecretary Sir Alexander Cadogan, Foreign Commissar Vyacheslav Molotov, and Ambassador Averell Harriman.

If These Rugs Could Talk!

5. King Ibn Saud, of Saudi Arabia, confers with President Franklin Roosevelt aboard the U.S.S. *Quincy.* Egypt 2/14/45. Admiral William Leahy is at left while Marine Corps Colonel Eddy is kneeling before the king.

President Franklin Roosevelt conferred with Amir Ibn Saud, of Saudia Arabia, aboard the U.S.S. *Quincy* on Valentine's day in 1945. FDR flew to this meeting in a four engine transfer plane (a VC-54 named the *Sacred Cow*), while King Saud sailed from his kingdom aboard the U.S. destroyer *Murphy*. Both leaders were in failing health, and FDR gave the King his spare wheelchair, one of the memorable diplomatic gifts exchanged on that day. Despite their use of wheelchairs, both leaders were careful not to be photographed in them.

In this scene, *khodrang* rugs appear upon the floor of the *Quincy*. The Persian word *khodrang* means self color, and these rugs are made with naturally colored wool, using no dyes. *Khodrang* rugs are brown, beige, black, gray, or white; the natural colors of camel, goat, and sheep hair from which these kilims, or flatweaves, are woven. The prominent rug in the photograph has a simple desert star design, creating a familiar sense of place for the visiting King Saud. This rug gives the ruler of the tribal kingdom of Arabia a feeling of home aboard this American military vessel. Whether the rugs were Navy issue, the inspired set design of an FDR aide, or the property of King Saud remains a mystery. However, there is no doubt that these rugs served an important function in this military, diplomatic event.

The historic meeting aboard the *Quincy* was the first time President Roosevelt met with the King of Arabia, and the first time serious discussion focused upon Arab-Jewish relations and the Palestine question. Roosevelt introduced his own fanciful topic, irrigation and cultivation of the Arabian Desert. King Saud dismissed Roosevelt's speculative inquiry, saying he had been a warrior all his life, not a farmer!

A wheelchair was not the only practical diplomatic gift given to the Saudi ruler aboard the *Quincy*. FDR also gave His Majesty a new antibiotic called penicillin. Ibn Saud's physician asked if it was good for venereal disease, and both doctor and king were impressed when the reply was affirmative!

If These Rugs Could Talk!

The meeting took place in the Renaissance Hall of Vizcaya, a glorious Florida villa, built in the Italian style by industrialist James Deering in 1916. The two world leaders had unlimited access to the palatial villa, with one *sic transit proviso* . . .

Pope and President were forbidden to walk upon the fine Hispano-Moresque armorial carpet, dating back to the 15th century, and bearing the coat of arms of two noble Spanish families.

Within the boundaries of Vizcaya, Carpets rule!

The Father of the American Foreign Service had come to England to witness the repeal of the noxious Stamp Act. Franklin told his wife he celebrated his joy by purchasing "A large true Turkey Carpet costing 10 Guineas for the Dining Room Parlor," one of the earliest references to oriental carpets in the American colonies.

Knowing Franklin's partiality to turkeys, one can only assume Deborah's joy was great when she learned that the carpet her husband brought home was **from** Turkey and, for the frugal Franklin, a bargain at 10 guineas!

General Norman Schwarzkopf, commander-in-chief of the U.S. Central Command, visited with now Emir Hamad bin Isa al-Khalifa of Bahrain in the days immediately following Allied success in the Gulf War. In the photograph both men are smiling, surely with satisfaction and relief, after the liberation of Kuwait from Iraqi occupation forces.

Schwarzkopf is the soldier returning victorious from the battlefield who practices carpet diplomacy with a member of the Gulf Cooperation Council (GCC). He is here to thank Bahrain for contributions to the Allied forces, which included combat aircraft, airfield landing privileges, and secret intelligence services concerning the demographics of Kuwait.

The general and emir stand upon a *Nain* carpet, clearly identifiable in the photograph by the characteristic field of curving patterns of flowering branches. A *Nain* is a quality carpet, often made of silk, with a high knot density. Is it a coincidence that, in this moment of military victory, the U.S. Army photographer features General Schwarzkopf's combat boots firmly planted upon the central medallion of this fine Persian carpet?

Operation Desert Storm is the first electronic war where cruise missiles and smart bombs were observed hitting long distance destinations with precision accuracy. Amidst the media coverage of high technology, one could frequently spy an oriental rug. Carpets appeared in diplomatic reception rooms, as well as in the tents of soldiers and refugees. Surely, if these rugs could talk, what stories they would tell us of valor, fear, suffering, and victory in this Middle Eastern conflict in the heart of oriental carpet country!

6. General Schwarzkopf and Lt. Gen. Hamad Bin Isa Al-Khalifa during a state visit to Bahrain.

Carpets In Diplomatic Space

Oriental rugs can be seen in diplomatic space throughout the world. A visit to the Embassy of Japan, in Washington, DC, rewards the eye with unique Japanese furnishings and accessories, but the entrance hallway contains a large Persian carpet. The Diplomatic Reception Rooms of the United States Department of State contain numerous oriental rugs complementing the collection of American decorative objects and furnishings. These rugs rotate regularly, appearing in different diplomatic rooms for the sake of preservation and variety. The most valuable rug in the State Department collection is a 28-foot *Bachtiari*, dating from 1800. This Eastern carpet is one of the oldest items within the State Department collection, and rug enthusiasts like to call it the early Eastern ambassador to Western diplomatic space.

Oriental rugs will continue to appear in diplomatic space. When sides are drawn in war and peace, trade, and state to state issues, resolution requires the right environment. Oriental rugs create that environment, providing an atmosphere that is both substantive and warm. Cast your eyes beyond the talking heads and signing hands, and seek the silent carpet underfoot. You will find it, rest assured.

| 7. *Kashan* carpet.

II Roll Out The Red Carpet!
Carpets in Privileged Space

Look into the Kashan carpet, a work that belongs in the hallways of the powerful and exalted. This carpet bespeaks ease with elegance, the reward of privilege. Floral abundance in colorful shades of spice fixes our attention. This carpet is a herald: Behold the Mighty!

Musical Suggestion: *Oriental March*, first movement of the *Aladdin Suite*, by Carl Nielsen

Come with me into privileged space. Through imposing doors of palaces, state houses, and corporate suites, we pass into the realm of power and authority. This is the place of kings, presidents, and professionals. For centuries oriental rugs have defined the privileged space of the noble, wealthy, and elite. Through the ages rugs were woven within court workshops of Persian, Ottoman, Mughal, Chinese, and French monarchs. To this day certain noble families reserve heirloom carpets for their coronations and weddings. Why do these time-honored carpet traditions exist?

King Henry VIII, a formidable symbol of power and authority, knew the value of a carpet underfoot to advance a commanding royal image. He is well deserving of the title "Carpet King," for he was the proud possessor of more than 500 carpets. Each was carefully recorded in his *Inventories* with categories for carpets of: "Turkey," "Venice," or "English making." These carpet entries include curious place descriptions for table, cupboard, window, bench, and floor.

Hans Holbein painted this portrait of Henry VIII as propaganda. Here is a ruler by divine right, and Holbein has constructed a monument to monarchy. His visual choices support this argument—ornamental clothing, massive physique, and that haughty gaze—demanding attention and respect. But most imperiously, the King proudly stands, colossus-like, upon an Anatolian *Ushak* carpet whose central medallion clearly defines his regal place.

King Henry is dressed in the high fashion of the Renaissance age in elaborate robes of silk, brocade, and fur. White fabric peeking out in the slit sleeves and shirt of the king is padding called bombast, puffing up the already corpulent look of the monarch. Our own contemporary associations with the word bombast include grandiosity or inflated style, associations that King Henry would surely have welcomed.

This monarch does not wear a crown, yet twin crowns appear on either side of his head in the decorative wall hanging. King Henry's imperial robes, jewels, aristocratic demeanor, and that rich carpet underfoot all serve his royal purpose. Clearly we are in the presence of a powerful king to be revered by loyalists, and feared by anyone who would dare to question his authority. Numerous portraits exist of King Henry in this characteristic full-body pose, refashioning the legitimacy of monarchy. In each painting the king is distinguished by standing with feet firmly planted upon a different oriental rug!

The projection of power and authority rendered through carpet associations is not exclusively reserved for western leaders. Even in the remote Kingdom of Bhutan carpets keep company with kings. The facing photograph features the Bhutanese king, Jigme Singye Wangchuck, meeting with ministers in the throne room while seated upon oriental carpets.

Bhutan, an ancient kingdom, is located at the foot of the Himalayas between China and India. It is named "Land of the Thunder Dragon" because of violent storms coming down from the peaks above. The country is a theocracy with a hereditary monarch presiding over temporal affairs. The king collaborates with the *je khenpo*, the Buddhist leader, in spiritual matters. Mahayana Buddhism is the official religion of the country, and deeply held beliefs have shaped the nation's history. Tradition continues to play a vital role in the remote Kingdom of Bhutan where one finds landscapes dotted with temples and fortified monasteries or *dzongs*. Citizens dress in robes called *ghos*, with a focused pursuit of virtue and transcendental wisdom, linking them with the tradition of ancestors. Archery is Bhutan's only Olympic sport, and the team consults an astrologer for assistance in selecting players and casting spells upon the opposition!

From this timeless world, we view a throne room with no time signature. The brocaded wall paintings, *thangkas*, the pride of a nation renowned for stunning textiles, could come from any period. Following ancient custom, the throne room floor is covered with floral design rugs, which provide a comfortable surface, visually pleasing design, and warmth for this alpine room. The current king sits under a canopy in a royal position elevated above his ministers, much as his ancestors have done. Since Bhutan is a theocracy, conducting the business of government is a prayerful practice. And so the rugs serve a higher purpose, defining meditative space in which a king and his ministers can calmly focus their thoughts on the pursuit of enlightened government.

Carpets have appeared in the throne rooms of caesars, tsars, shahs, rajahs, sultans, emperors, kings, and mandarins in kingdoms near and far. While the attributed significance of throne carpets will vary according to the culture of a country, the oriental rug is ever present in regal space providing majestic beauty, splendid comfort, and even sequestered enlightenment!

Roll Out The Red Carpet!

How intimidating it is to be summoned for a reprimand within the carpeted space of authority!
Carpets bring dignity AND project superiority.
Sometimes, it is not what is said, but where.

Carpets In Privileged Space

Sixth century Sassanian King Chosroes commissioned the legendary *Spring Carpet* to keep himself ever mindful of the season. A garden design of flowers, trees, and streams was woven of gold and silver threads, with silk and precious stones.

Centuries later, in a kingdom far away, Philadelphia industrialist Fairman Rogers wanted his Victorian "cottage" in Newport to display something of the glitz and glory of his own Gilded Age and . . . **Only a garden to remind him of a carpet would do!**

Rogers had a magnificent Persian garden carpet hauled out to the lawn of his estate, instructing the army of gardeners to reproduce in landscape what was woven in wool. The result was a giant natural carpet that never needed shelter from rain!

Oriental rugs appear in offices of lawyers, corporate executives, and physicians seeking to communicate a sense of authority, prosperity, and good taste. Sigmund Freud was a legendary collector of antiquities, which he found were a fitting metaphor for psychoanalysis, a method he described as "digging into the past." *Heriz* and *Tabriz* carpets appear in Freud's professional office. However, it is the one covering his couch, the *Shiraz,* which has become the icon of modern psychiatry.

This *Shiraz* rug dates from about 1910 and was possibly woven by tribal nomads of the Khamseh Confederacy from the Fars province of Iran. The field contains diamond-shaped medallions and borders, characteristic designs of the *Shiraz* carpet. Lustrous patina and the soft texture of this rug seem to invite us to recline upon it. Think of the many patients who lay supine upon this rug telling stories about the pattern, texture, and fabric of their own lives in waking hours and in dreamland. Is it not curious that Dr. Freud placed his patients upon a nomadic rug filled with tribal signs and symbols as he helped them to interpret dreams and confront their own personal demons?

Freud's followers have imitated the method of the father of modern psychiatry by placing patients upon a couch during psychoanalysis. Therapists also follow Freud's example in the placement of a chair at the head of the couch. This recommended arrangement prevents distractions from direct eye contact, allowing the patient to focus freely and the therapist to concentrate solely upon the spoken word. Yet how many therapists imitate the example of Dr. Freud by placing their patients upon a rug covered couch?

Freud characterized the road to self-knowledge as "meandering and labyrinthine, like the arabesque tracery in a carpet." Why Dr. Freud chose oriental rugs as an integral part of his professional space is a fascinating question. Could it be that these rugs not only provided pleasing aesthetic beauty and physical comfort, but even psychic relief for Freud's patients? Whether one stands, sits, or rests, a carpet can touch the mind and the body in untold ways.

11. Freud's couch.

United States history has never included a pedigree of titled royalty, yet America sustains corporate barons and merchant princesses whose entrepreneurial spirit has earned them respect, fame, and fortune. For this privileged class of Americans, the oriental is often the carpet of choice. Such was the case with Mrs. John Jacob Astor, who held the title "Queen of the Four Hundred" because of the famous annual ball of New York high society which she hosted in her home for 400 guests. When Mrs. Astor was questioned on why she had not invited certain socially registered individuals in the rug trade to her celebrated dinner, she replied: "I buy my rugs from them, but is that any reason why I should invite them to walk on them?"

By the final decades of the nineteenth century, oriental rugs were standard furnishing for first-class parlor suites on Mississippi steamboats, Baltimore railway cars, and transatlantic oceanliners. Mark Twain customarily sat in an armchair upon an oriental rug during his famous public readings across the United States. Hal Holbrook has continued Twain's rug tradition in contemporary impersonations of the master. It has been reported that Holbrook would not perform without an oriental carpet underfoot!

Oprah Winfrey is a successful contemporary woman whose talents have securely placed her within the ranks of the privileged. She has earned recognition as a popular talk show host, Hollywood actress, and chief executive of a thriving corporate conglomerate. Her book discussion group is a global conversation. If you were to place the "Queen of Talk" upon an oriental rug, what would you choose?

Carpets In Privileged Space

Oriental rugs serve the privileged in powerful places when the image of competence and authority needs to be defined. Potent carpet associations prevail across centuries and cultures. Carpets can pronounce the majesty of a Tudor king, promote the stature of a newly elected president, or perpetuate the hallowed traditions of Eastern ancestors. No longer the exclusive reserve of a noble elite, oriental rugs are now accessible to discriminating buyers from all walks of life. Whether these carpets appear in palace halls, corporate boardrooms, or professional workspaces, they project a formidable image for those who walk and work upon them. Wise are they who choose to privilege themselves with such magnificent possessions!

12. *Bijar* carpet.

III From Cradle to Grave!
Carpets in Domestic Space

Look into the Bijar carpet. This rug belongs in domestic space. Its geography imitates the landscape of a family. There is impressive unity, but slowly we become aware of diversity. Each section, like members in a family, stands alone in well-proportioned patterns within clearly defined boundaries. This carpet invites use. Once upon this rug we become a community: sprawling, reading, playing games, watching the fire, or listening to music. The rug is the heart of our home.

♪ Musical Suggestion: *Arabesque No. I in E Major*, by Claude Debussy

ow we come home to domestic space. Here oriental rugs serve as silent witness to the tender times in our private lives. It is here that rugs have a powerful potential to provoke thought and feeling. Carpets can precipitate memory, connecting us nostalgically to past experience: a scent, a sound, a touch. With carpets at home in our daily lives, the special becomes the unforgettable: birthdays, engagements, anniversaries. Rugs also reach to our future, a rich inheritance bearing witness to meaningful family traditions and storing for us a treasure of legacy. No single possession holds so much of our unwritten history.

Pause now and you will recall some special family happenings that have occurred upon your oriental rug. Perhaps you remember the first steps of a toddler or the wide-eyed wonderment of a child unwrapping holiday gifts on a richly patterned field. Can you see a timid adolescent adjusting a prom corsage or a nervous bride arranging her veil for prenuptial photos upon floral borders? Yes, there are poignant moments too on a carpet. Times when tears were shed over a lost love or reconciliation was made at a family reunion. Our oriental rugs witness these tender times in our lives. They possess the evocative power to rekindle recollections of these once-upon-a-time happenings that have made us who we are.

As adults we associate sense memories with rugs from childhood. What places in your heart hold memories of special moments you have spent upon a rug? Why not begin now to recollect these special times in your life? A magic carpet is not necessary to transport you to another place; untold joy can be found by imaginatively engaging with the figures within the carpet in your own home.

Carpets In Domestic Space

13. Girl on *Mahal* carpet.

A woman from Philadelphia remembers amusing herself as a child by imagining the scent of roses, carnations, and lilies so vividly figured in the *Kerman* carpet of her living room.
Roses, carnations, and lilies?
Not only are those scents alive in her memory, but today,
with the carpet her father bequeathed to her, Pat can still *smell the roses*.

Carpets In Domestic Space

𝒜nd was there a time when you could trace the intricate meanderings in your carpet with your finger, unlocking the hidden key to its design?

A man from Virginia recalls happy times spent as a young boy in his father's study,
quietly racing his toy trucks around the many borders of a *Bokhara* rug.
Then, his father's feet, the legs of the desk, and the paw of the lampstand
formed with that rich, ruby red carpet a complex landscape that he alone could traverse.
Today, he finds himself still tracing those long forgotten routes on the same carpet now in his study.

From Cradle To Grave!

With his son's son protected in his lap, a grandfather from New York brings a *Tabriz* hunting carpet to life.
The grandfather names the nameless beasts lurking in the foliage.
Just as his father had done for him.
Safe in his grandfather's lap, the child creates his version of the never-ending tale.

Carpets In Domestic Space

Two figures stand upon the Caucasian carpet in the courtyard of Coburg Castle in 1894. We are looking at the soon-to-be Tsar Nicholas II of the House of Romanov and Princess Alexandra of Hesse-Darmstadt on their engagement day. The rug they stand upon might be called a betrothal rug in this official photograph outside the home of the intended bride. While the carpet formally speaks of the dignity and distinction of the royal couple, it also tenderly tells of the intimacy of their domestic event.

This dynastic marriage between the heir to the Russian throne and the grand daughter of English Queen Victoria was a true love match. In their time, the young couple attracted global media attention. In our time, a century after their match was made, this royal pair has continued to captivate public imagination in popular biographies and museum exhibitions. How appropriate it is that the engaged couple stands upon an oriental rug, for both royals owned a vast collection of carpets through family inheritance. This was truly a royal rug match of the grandest design!

14. Nicholas and Alexandra on their engagement day.

From Cradle To Grave!

15. Dowry rug. *Konya*, 17th century.

Carpets In Domestic Space

Rugs and marriage share a history together. Carpets accent the life cycle of a family from birth to death, cradle to grave. In weaving cultures, rugs given to a baby girl eventually become part of her dowry. As a condition for marriage, a maiden may be required to display her rug weaving ability to a prospective groom. Prowess at the loom increases a woman's personal status, respect, and even her bride price! Rugs remain a dominant presence within any home, and even a companion in death to cover a coffin or adorn a mausoleum.

Oriental rugs weave together economics, culture, and the personal lives of individuals. A dowry or *kis* (the word means maiden or bride in Turkish) rug is a tender example. Looking into a *kis* rug, one sees the signature of a maiden vividly marking simple and subtle thoughts of marriage through the grammar of design. The rug captures woven images expressing the dreams, expectations, and anxieties of the maiden approaching matrimony.

Engaging in fanciful reverie (and courageous speculation!) about the supposed identity of the weaver of this antique dowry carpet, I happened to recollect a Persian quotation, which translates: "When I finish weaving my carpet, I will propose to my . . . *Wife!*" Can a marriage rug assume a masculine or a feminine personality? Could the symbolism within this marriage rug express the hoped-for-desires of a bride*groom*? Figures appearing within the carpet take on new meaning when viewed with a gendered eye!

Kocboynuzu, ram's horn, is the masculine symbol of fertility. The main border is composed of small squares suggesting fertility and abundance.

Hair band implies the desire for marriage. Rose indicates the purity of love. Dragon and eye motifs are used with protective purposes.

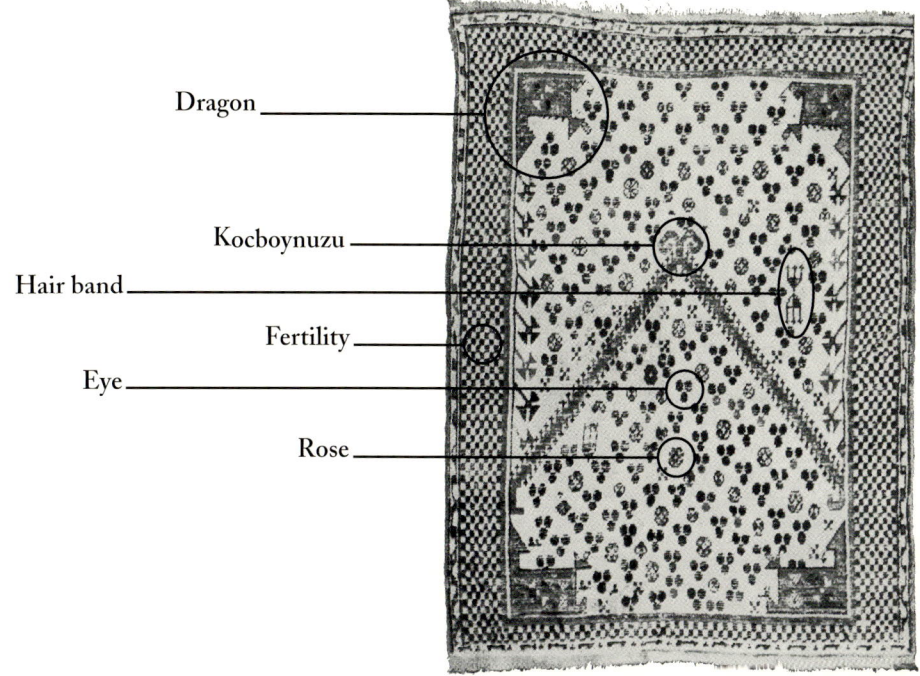

From Cradle To Grave!

In the human life cycle, the fruit of love is pregnancy and birth. The facing carpet is a pregnancy prayer rug containing symbols of fertility and protection. The ewer, goose feet, pomegranate, and tree of life are commonly found within the design of pregnancy rugs.

This antique rug is badly worn, not an uncommon condition for a rug more than 300 years old. Yet, is it not curious that the wear marks of this rug occur in locations where the devout petitioner might place knees, head, and hands? Could it be that what we see are the genuine signs of *prayer?* Perhaps the worn spots mark the place where a woman prayed her heart's intention for protection of her baby and herself. One can only wonder how many babies were prayed over upon this very rug.

This is a prayer rug woven by a pregnant woman. The wide border is decorated with rose and carnation motifs. In Anatolia the ewer suggests water which in turn symbolizes fertility and respect. The ewer is also a symbol of pregnancy. The tree of life motif continues in the lower parts of the rug, expressing the weaver's wish that the baby will lead a happy life. The goose feet and the dragon motifs are used to ensure protection for the mother and child in case of any danger during birth.

Carpets In Domestic Space

16. Pregnancy rug. *Konya*, 17th century.

17. Aged by the makeup wizards of Hollywood, Geraldine Fitzgerald, Laurence Olivier, Leo G. Carroll, and Flora Robson appear in this 1939 Samuel Goldwyn version of Emily Bronte's *Wuthering Heights*.

Carpets In Domestic Space

Nothing can match the welcoming presence of an oriental rug before a blazing hearth fire, the classic image of nostalgic greeting cards and fond associations of warmth and security. Yet look at the facing page, a still from the 1939 production of *Wuthering Heights*. The icy glares of the four protagonists are bone chilling, straining the ability even of a hearth rug, blazing fire, and canine to provide warmth and cheery camaraderie. How sad!

Hearth rugs are purposefully made to enlarge agreeable architectural space. For centuries, *ojakbashi* rugs ("hearth-head" in Turkish) were woven by Turkoman tribes in a U shape to surround nomadic fireplaces, increasing the welcoming space.

Hearth rugs have been linked to sacred obligations of hospitality. Stories are told of *ojakbashi* rugs defining the place of refuge within a nomadic tent. While standing upon a hearth rug, even a hostile enemy must be given protection by a host. The code of hospitality and welcome cannot be violated upon a hearth rug, even by Heathcliff. Hatred and dissention accede to a higher priority of bounteous courtesy within space defined by the hearth rug!

A lesson might be learned from ancient wisdom and tribal custom. Feuding families who now experience painful holiday gatherings could benefit from the practice of hearth rug amnesty. In certain families, a reminder of this custom has served as the invitation to dialogue. For some lucky people, a rug has ultimately served as the place of forgiveness and reconciliation within a family. These are the individuals who understand the meaning of Edgar Allan Poe's words, "The soul of the apartment is in the carpet!"

18. *Ispahan* carpet.

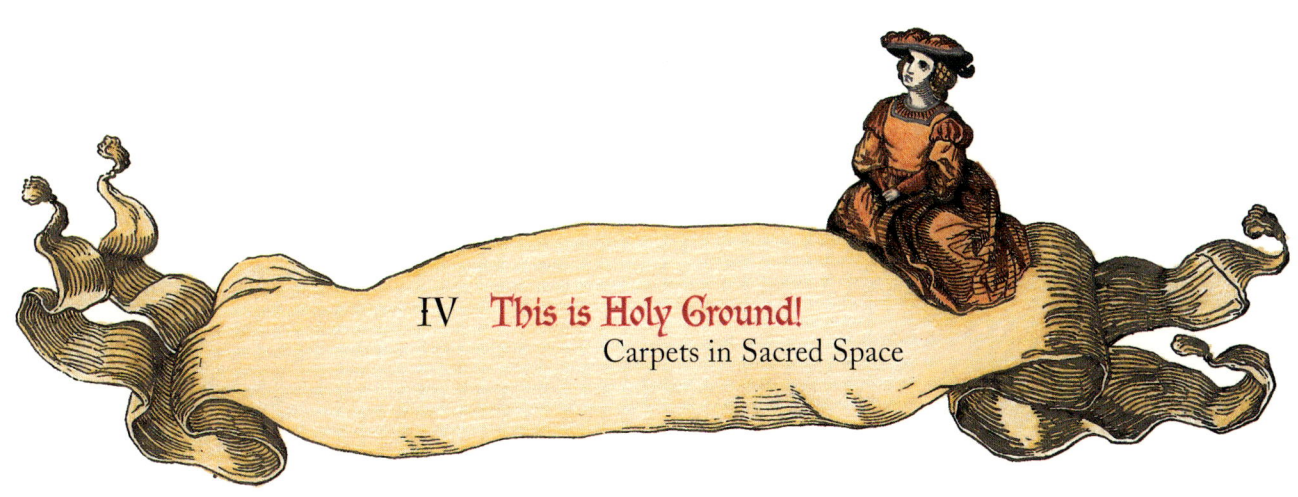

IV This is Holy Ground!
Carpets in Sacred Space

Look into the Ispahan carpet, gaze into the eye of the all-seeing God.
Here we sense the presence of the divine, watchful and welcoming.
One is drawn to the sacred geometry, witness to the endless variety of the Almighty.
On this rug our thoughts are rapt in reverence and awe.

♪ Musical Suggestion: *Sanctus*, in *Requiem*, Op. 48, by Gabriel Fauré

This Is Holy Ground!

et us enter into sacred space. This is the holy ground of mosques, churches, synagogues and temples. Oriental rugs have a hallowed history in places of worship of all three People of the Book: Jews, Christians, and Moslems. Carpets are associated with symbols of holiness and appear in the company of Buddha, Confucius, Hindu deities, the Star of David, the Crescent, the Holy Trinity, and the Virgin Mary. Early reformist John Calvin, eschewing icons, religious paintings, and stained glass, considered oriental carpets fitting adornment in Protestant churches.

In Islam, prayer rugs are more than adornment. They serve a devotional purpose to assist faithful believers performing compulsory prayer, or *salat*. This second of the five pillars of Islam is a solemn obligation fulfilled five times each day: dawn, noon, mid-afternoon, evening, and night. Compulsory prayer must occur on a clean spot, which a prayer rug provides. Every Friday at noon, communal prayer takes place in the mosque. In the facing photograph, taken in the Selimiye Mosque, the vast congregation sits upon oriental rugs. They all face the *mihrab*, the prayer niche of the mosque directed towards Mecca. Ornamental arabesques and calligraphy with sacred words of the Koran appear in the mosaics on the ceiling dome and walls of the mosque, mirroring designs and inscriptions found within oriental rugs.

Turks use the word *ciddi*, meaning serious, to describe rugs in a mosque. These are sober rugs, many given as votive offerings in memory of a loved one. The congregation at prayer becomes a spiritual community uniting the intentions of the living with the memory of the deceased upon whose rugs they pray. The holy ground of sacred space is the place of spiritual transcendence.

Carpets In Sacred Space

19 Worshippers in Selimiye Mosque in Edirne, Turkey.

Ettore Cercone's painting, *Evening Prayer*, is a visual narrative of faithful Muslims performing evening *salat*. We are on a rooftop with the silhouette of domes and minarets in the distance. Two men pray in prescribed positions upon prayer rugs. One is prostrate in humble submission, the other sits with extended arms and open palms acknowledging acceptance of the will of the Creator.

The women, alone and in stillness, are engaged in their own private reverie. We observe with each of the four figures a moment of separation and communion. The painter describes the unique awareness and connection each figure experiences. They are detached from one another and from us, but attached to a greater force, the Almighty.

This painting makes us aware of a sacred focus which oriental rugs bring to the spiritual encounter between God and man. There is a reverential silence communicated here in the painting reminding us that this time of prayer is an *awe-full* moment. Prayer rugs are created to facilitate this moment.

For a devout weaver, work at the loom is holy labor fulfilling solemn obligation. Often prayer rugs are woven accompanied by song or spoken prayer with each knot tied to the greater glory of Allah. Linger here awhile; listen to the music of Faure's *Sanctus*, and experience your own sacred moment.

20. *Evening Prayer,* Ettore Cercone, 1893.

This Is Holy Ground!

21. Synagogue rug, Cairo, early seventeenth century.

Carpets In Sacred Space

At first glance, the Ottoman carpet we see here, with pillars of wisdom and central arch, might be identified as another Islamic prayer rug. But this is a Jewish carpet bearing the Hebrew inscription of Psalm 118:20, "This is the Gate of the Lord through which the righteous shall enter." The field contains a Hanukkah lamp, an eight-branched candelabra and master light. This is a knotted *parokhet*, a rug used in a synagogue as an Ark curtain to guard the Torah. It is a rug to be walked upon in thought, not on foot.

A Jewish carpet facing Jerusalem is called *mizrach*, the Hebrew word for orient or east. It serves as a directional finder to the Holy City. The origins of directional prayer are as old as the ancient Egyptians who built their sanctuaries facing the south, towards the source of the Nile. For the Jews, directional prayer towards the east began when Solomon built the First Temple of the Israelites in Jerusalem, facing the east. Talmudic instructions advise all Jewish believers to direct their prayers towards Jerusalem.

In the twelfth century, the famous philosopher Maimonides exempted carpets from the prohibition of Jewish Law against graven images. Nevertheless, Maimonides would close his eyes while at prayer in the synagogue to prevent distractions from carpets hanging on the walls.

The Talmudic rule of *hiddur mitzvah* prescribes the duty to make ritual objects as beautiful as possible, and this rule has been applied to justify figural representations appearing within Jewish carpets. These carpets are found in synagogues and temples throughout the world and their beauty witnesses to the faith and skill of their makers.

Here we see in a photograph where an oriental rug serves a sacred ceremonial function in the Roman Catholic tradition. An altar table rests upon the rug during this mass celebrated by Pope John Paul II while visiting his Polish homeland in Gdansk in 1987. A crowd of 750,000 attended the liturgy taking place upon a temporary stage in an outdoor arena. The *Kashan* rug serves to define holy ground for this vast multitude.

At the gathering, the pope voiced his particular intention for the mass saying, "I pray for the special heritage of Polish solidarity." The pope's prayers were obviously heard, for his visit in no small way contributed to the once thought unbelievable success of the Polish Solidarity movement in 1989.

Carpets In Sacred Space

22. Pope John Paul II at Gdansk, Poland, in 1987.

57

This Is Holy Ground!

Historical inventories of many houses of worship include entries for carpets that are splendidly displayed, but only on special occasions. Here we see one of the red carpets of the Vatican rolled out for a remarkable sacramental event. Amidst the magnificence of St. Peter's Basilica in Rome, seventy men receive Holy Orders to the priesthood upon a massive 180 by 100 foot carpet.

The ceremony takes place in the heart of the holiest place in the basilica. For these priests lying fully prostrate upon a crimson and gold brocade carpet, this ordination is an unparalleled mark of distinction. The new priests recite the Litany of the Saints invoking saintly assistance in fulfilling their priestly calling.

The act of full prostration is at once a vivid acknowledgment of submission to God and a surrender of former habits for the new responsibilities of pastoral service to the people of God.

The carpet lies upon the marble pavement of the basilica, a powerful witness to the solemnity of this sacramental ceremony. In the vast Vatican collection, the carpet is just one piece. Here in this inspirational place it majestically serves the sacred.

23. Ordination ceremony inside the Vatican.

Carpets In Sacred Space

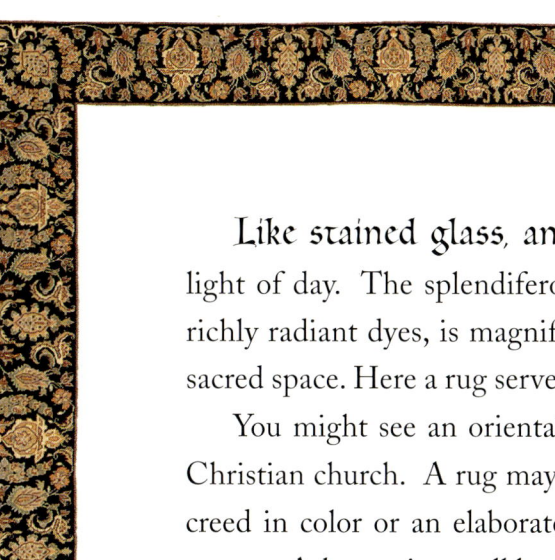

Like stained glass, an oriental carpet glows with the ever-changing light of day. The splendiferous quality of an oriental rug, with silky surface and richly radiant dyes, is magnificently evident when a flood of natural light invades sacred space. Here a rug serves as a lucent profession of God as Light of the World.

You might see an oriental rug in an octagonal Islamic mosque or a cruciform Christian church. A rug may depict mihrab, cross, or menorah, speaking a modest creed in color or an elaborate testimony of sublime spirituality. Rugs may serve as Ark curtains, wall hangings, altar rests, or prayer seats within holy places. No matter what the creed or practice of the congregation, a rug will be there as helpful companion defining holy ground in the sacred encounter between God and man.

24. *Kerman* carpet.

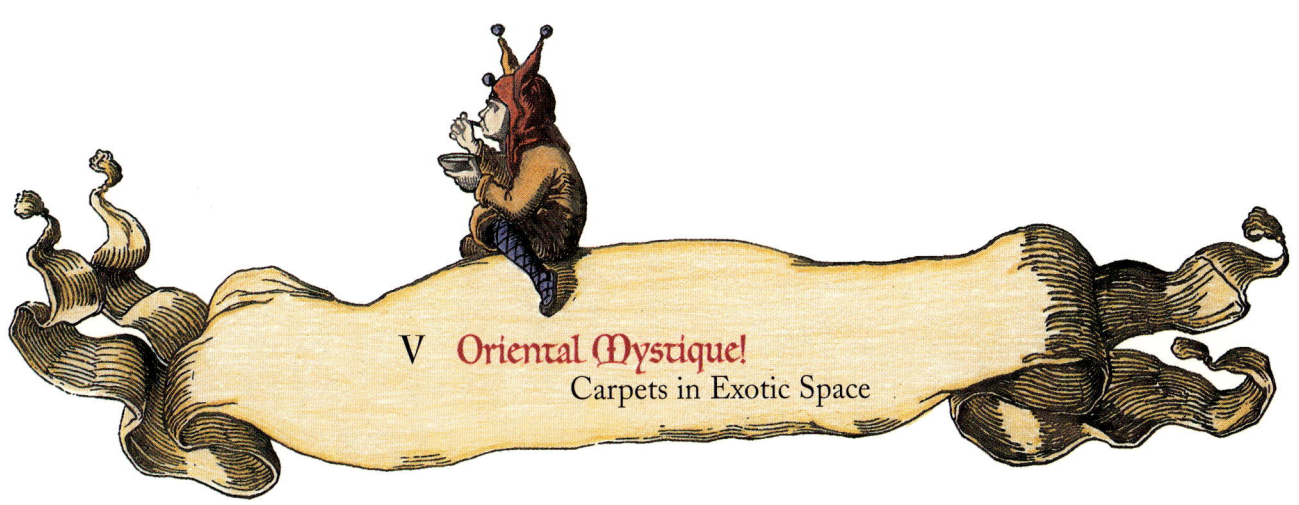

V Oriental Mystique!
Carpets in Exotic Space

Look into this Kerman carpet so evocative of exotic space.

The carpet calls us to the unconventional.

Through it we are bidden to abandon restraint and surrender to sensuality.

In exotic space, the senses lead, the spirit follows.

Musical Suggestion: *In a Persian Market*, by Albert Ketèlbey

Oriental Mystique!

ove with me to exotic space. From the known world we move to the home of myth and mystery, where oriental carpets are identified with the sensual and mysterious. Carpet appreciation in the West has been wed to orientalism, a study of and fixation with Eastern life and philosophy. To Western romantics, orientalism has always represented an earthly paradise, a place of escape, released inhibitions, and amorous languor. And carpets lie at the heart of this paradise.

Imagine Cleopatra, wrapped in a fine oriental rug, rendered unto Caesar—a grand entrance earning Cleopatra a Caesar as lover and ally. Her carpet conquest continues with Mark Antony, and the oriental rug becomes an established attribute of compelling feminine attraction.

Long is the list of celebrated stage and screen beauty queens seeking to capture the exotic glamour of the Egyptian temptress in a carpet. Here is a publicity photograph of Theda Bara (the Vamp whose name is an anagram for "Arab Death") playing Cleopatra in 1918. This sultry Queen of the Nile embodies exotica from the winged crown on top of her head to the asp at the tip of her ankle. Cleopatra is an ancient "material girl" whose sensuality is physically defined through sumptuous textiles. Her accessories—a revealing robe, silk-seated throne, and rug underfoot—become Cleopatra's attributes. This *femme fatale* inhabits an ornate, prohibited, alien world far removed from the ordinary life we know. Quintessentially oriental! There is mystery and intrigue in the exotic carpeted space Cleopatra occupies, beckoning with sensual, evocative allure.

25. Theda Bara as Cleopatra.

Oriental Mystique!

𝔐ythical women have their marvelous carpet tales to tell. In Homer's Odyssey, the weaving sorceress Circe is believed to possess the power of enchantment, turning men into animals. Yet, she is beguiled by her love of Ulysses. Will that love make her mortal? In this Claudio Bravo painting, we visit Circe's moment of decision. We view an erotic, exotic woman revealing just enough flesh to convince us that she is temptingly human and vulnerable. How beautiful is her face in profile, alluring flesh, and the shapely arm, leg, and hip. Who can resist the charm of that fuchsia turban wrapped about her head, sensuously floating down the back?

In the painting, Circe is seated in the company of *six* domesticated animals, perhaps all changelings: a sleeping dog and cat, a canary, guinea pig, parrot and rooster. Yet she holds the photograph of a man in one hand and a fruit pierced with *seven* pins in the other. Who will be the seventh changeling caught in the web of enchantment? Is it the man in the photograph she holds or could it even be Circe herself?

The oriental rug in this setting has both decorative and symbolic significance. The artist leaves nothing to chance. His choice of Circe's remarkable pose—one foot tiptoeing upon the blue field of the central medallion—and his selection of hexagonal shapes and pendants in richly varied hues, all lend a mysterious quality to the painting. Circe is stepping into something new and unknown, and her tenuous body language tells us she is uncertain. The dog sleeps upon the carpet, the rooster seems oblivious, but Circe is thoughtfully aware and wary.

The vanishing point in the painting leads to the sharp corner in the far right. Circe is literally cornered in the scene on canvas and in her own life. Like the plush velvet couch upon which she rests, Circe could yield to the man in the photograph. And like the marked abrash, or color change in the carpet, she could change her own colors. Her life altered forever. The moment is at hand.

We viewers come to the painting as uninvited guests with the privileged opportunity to gaze upon a mythic, feminine icon in a vulnerable moment of truth. Like Cleopatra, Circe has direct physical contact with her oriental rug, which results in a sensual presence greater than the sum of the pair. Circe's charms join with the mystery in her carpet in a mutually enhancing union, creating an unforgettable carpet legend in canvas.

26. *Circe*, Claudio Bravo, 1986.

This Flashdance photograph of Jennifer Beals defines contradictions of late twentieth century women. Fashion verses anti-fashion, dependence verses freedom, and sensuality verses restraint. Beals wears jewels and high heel shoes, but a torn sweatshirt. She sits upon tasseled cushions reminiscent of a harem, but strikes a starkly independent pose.

And most particularly, eyes that beckon,
but arms which say, NO!

Beals is linked with the siren sisterhood of Circe and Cleopatra. In these three portraits, the carpet amplifies eroticism, enhances allure, and commands attention. The sultry icons on carpets characterize and fix the boundaries of exotic space, for their times.

In ours, the *Flashdance* rug serves the same purpose. The carpet underfoot is the only object in the photograph with rich multi-color and clear definition. The rest of the scene consists of hazy forms in murky tones. It is the carpet that provides a solid foundation, on the floor, the place where this flashdancer comes alive and makes things happen.

What a feeling!

Carpets In Exotic Space

27. Jennifer Beals in *Flashdance*.

Oriental Mystique!

28. Gertrude Vanderbilt and friends at an oriental feast.

Carpets In Exotic Space

Here is a portrait of Gertrude Vanderbilt, accompanied by turbaned male companions in seraglio attire, hosting one of her legendary orientalist soirees in Paris, 1913. A legendary scion of American wealth, Ms. Vanderbilt wears a harem costume by Leon Bakst, famed designer for the Ballet Russe. This era is the heyday of orientalism in the Western world when ballets such as *Firebird, Cleopatra, Scheherazade,* and *Salome* were an international rage. These orientalist ballets inspired the most fantastic Western recreations of the East with odalisques, sultans, and slaves pursuing forbidden love in prohibited places.

For Gertrude Vanderbilt, the romance of the East was irresistible. Her own sensuality and eroticism bloomed while living in Paris. At the feast, Gertrude embraces oriental fantasy with rich *Tabriz* carpets on the ground. Other exotic textiles canopy the ceiling, hang upon the walls, and cover the table and pillows upon which her guests recline. The kaleidoscopic effect of fashion, fantasy and furnishings must have been intoxicating in living color!

Perhaps this privileged Vanderbilt woman wanted to make life imitate art at this feast with her male harem in her opulent, fantasy world. We can view this Arabian Nights scene without listening to Rimsky-Korsakov's *Scheherazade,* but we hear it anyway.

Oriental Mystique!

𝔉𝔣 𝔬𝔫𝔢 𝔠𝔞𝔯𝔭𝔢𝔱 𝔱𝔯𝔞𝔫𝔰𝔣𝔬𝔯𝔪𝔰, 𝔞 𝔴𝔞𝔩𝔩 𝔬𝔣 𝔱𝔥𝔢𝔪 𝔢𝔵𝔞𝔩𝔱𝔰. This carpet-covered wall of the ksaar of Maadid awaits the visit of Morocco's minister of culture. To Western eyes the scene is surreal, with carpets magically standing at attention. But to those familiar with Middle Eastern customs, this is a scene of ostentatious hospitality for which a wall of carpets is thoroughly appropriate. Herein stands the dichotomy of carpet appreciation: to the Westerner, carpets speak of the exotic, sensual, and mysterious, to the Easterner, of hospitality and tribute. The two spectators in this scene witness a bold display of prudent hospitality serving as a flattering tribute to a dignitary, as well as a colorful exhibition of regional craftsmanship.

The red rugs with vigorous geometric designs are similar in size. They work together, an army of woven wool, providing a striking visual contrast against the solid sandstone building. The street is stark and flat, yet the building dressed in carpets, illuminated in sunlight against vivid blue sky, is breathtaking to behold. All the elements in the photograph are natural, including the rugs. Even Aladdin on his carpet could not match the magic of a moment such as this when rugs, sun, sky, and sandstone join together to create an unforgettable natural wonder!

Carpets In Exotic Space

29. A wall of carpets in Maadid, Morocco.

Oriental Mystique!

Emile Delpree's portrait explores conflicting themes of The Warrior, a legendary orientalist figure. Occidental associations with the eastern warrior conjure up fearsome thoughts of a swarthy, ruthless, focused-and-invincible barbarian engaging in acts of plunder and pillage. From the Eastern perspective, the warrior is an independent, fearless-and-disciplined conqueror who proudly claims victory. Genghis Khan and Tamerlane are two brazen examples of such legendary warriors, and we can well imagine their tents filled with oriental carpets.

There is a mysterious ambiguity about the warrior in this painting who is both of this world and the next. Is he a guardian-protector of a home, mercenary soldier, or faithful fighter in a holy war? The weapons of his profession are visible: a rifle at his back with sheathed sword by his side. Yet the weapons are not in ready position, and this warrior is remarkably relaxed with a caftan casually open at the neck.

Look closely at the cross-footed stance of this figure. Is he leaning against the Turkish *Mudjar* prayer rug at his back? The warrior is curiously centered within the niche of the prayer rug. The lamp above his head and shoeless pose hint of holy purpose. Could it be that this warrior is centered, directed in passion and purpose to a higher cause which allows him to rest focused and fearless? Or perhaps what we see here is a relaxed warrior whose brash self-assurance makes him oblivious of concern for personal safety.

There is an expression pertaining to Turkish rugs, "A Turk's eye is on the red." Madder, a wild root producing a warm red dye, is the Turkish red in question. Delpree has artfully captured this Turkish red pigment in paint in the solid field of the prayer rug and in the numerous flickers of flame within its borders. This painting vividly illustrates how an oriental rug changes the environment it touches. Here bare stones and solid wall are transformed into beautifully textured surfaces, both fascinating to behold and mysterious to contemplate.

30. *The Warrior,* Emile Delpree (1850-1896).

Carpets In Exotic Space

Things oriental will continue to provoke associations with the exotic be they warriors in an uncertain cause, women behind veils, or queens in carpets. Eastern carpets with sumptuous texture, enchanting color, and beguiling design have the power to transform ordinary surroundings into extraordinary places. These carpets provide space for imaginative fantasy and physical comfort, seducing us to relax and abandon care. Nothing can match the power of carpets to render ambiguity and sensuality, the inscrutable and exotic core of Eastern allure so captivating to Western imagination.

31. *Tabriz* carpet.

VI Carpe T Diem!
Carpets in Unexpected Space

Look into the Tabriz carpet. A riotous assortment of stripes, checks and florabunda.

Celestial navigation! We are under the playful influence of carpet rage.

Rugs can elevate, transfix, relax, and excite.

They can also take you to unexpected places, like . . .

♪ Musical Suggestion: Overture, *Candide*, by Leonard Bernstein

Carpet Diem!

**eize the day and hold fast!**
We now enter the world of unpredictability to the undiscovered country of Carpet Diem! As juvenile author Dr. Seuss might say:

> What wonder you find
> When you come to this space
> Discover a rug
> In a never seen place!

Expect the extraordinary in this playful territory where uncommon carpets can make you laugh, cry, and think the unthinkable. Anything is possible in the land of Carpet Diem!

Rugs are born just like humans. They are woven, clipped, released from the loom, and carried to fresh water for cleansing. No baby likes the first bath, baby rugs included. As the picture shows, runaway rugs must be held in place. Rugs are like children, requiring hang time in the sun. They need grooming, shearing, and combing. Rugs like looking their best; with children it's less certain.

A rug's life, like our own, is not without peril. Rugs may bleed when fugitive dyes invade the territory of an adjacent color. White knots bring dandruff, and wear causes unwelcome wrinkles. But the gravest assault comes to the living carpet from moths and dry rot. Life is not easy for carpets who serve us so well. Yet rugs can be restored and made new, whole, and beautiful again. Oh, to be a carpet—mended, moisturized, and reborn, ready to serve the next generation!

Carpets In Unexpected Space

32. Weaver washing a rug in Iran.

Carpet Diem!

33. *Seeteppich*, or "Salty Carpet."

In 1996, Christie's auctioned this famous Seeteppich, the sea-carpet, from the collection of the Bernheimer family of Germany. It has a remarkable history. The story goes that this *Agra* carpet, woven for Victoria as empress of India, had a "sea change." At the dock in India, the massive rug measuring 18 by 49 feet, broke loose and plunged to the bottom of the harbor. The retrieved rug was not the original; salt water reacting with the blue dye created a pattern deemed unsuitable for the queen. Notwithstanding, the Bernheimer family purchased the carpet. A century later at the 1996 auction, the *Seeteppich* showed itself anything but an outcast when it changed hands at 25,000 British pounds (approximately $40,000).

Which proves? A sea-dunked carpet can become a sunken treasure!

You may ask, what is the point of a carpet on a beach? Or children wearing white shoes and frilly dresses at the seashore? And what ritual requires rug reverence? The point is that these are the children of the Russian tsar, Romanov grand duchesses tended by ladies-in-waiting. For royalty such as this, even a beach requires a *Caucasian* rug. A decade earlier, Nicholas and Alexandra, the parents of these children, pledged their troth on a similar carpet (page 41). Clearly royalty and their rugs cannot be separated!

Carpets In Unexpected Space

34. Russian beach scene with carpet in early 1900.

Clara Bow, idol of the Jazz Age. The It girl, exuberant, uninhibited, and lovable. Songwriter Sigmund Romberg captured her as "that improper fraction, of vague attraction, that gets the action, somehow." Here *It* is, as Bubbles, the heroine of *Red Hair*, striking an altogether familiar pose. Why familiar?

Cast a glance back to page 23 to engage in dueling poses. Dapper Henry VIII imperiously dons extravagant clothing making him the model of his age; flapper Bow indignantly doffs clothing and, nearly naked, becomes the model of hers. In similar settings both assume the gartered look, toe-forward, with cloth-of-honor draperies and an oriental rug underfoot. But more than four centuries separate the intention and impact of these two foils.

While Henry defines stature, dignity, and regal authority from his use of tapestry and carpet, Bubbles mocks that authority with comic effect. Garishly designed drapery is her cloth-of-honor, and that hunch-shouldered, gape-mouthed look of surpise clashes sharply with Henry's splendid strength. Compromise and vulnerability in contrast to awe and superiority. Can we ever again look at one and not think fondly of the other?

Carpets In Unexpected Space

35. Clara Bow, the *It* girl, in *Red Hair* in 1928.

Carpet Diem!

Now to a Carpet Diem conundrum, an antique shop serendipity, which continues to remain a haunting mystery. The print is dated 1893, but it lacks a title. There is no information about the setting, the situation, or the figures within the carpet scene. What is going on here? Are we witnessing a healing service or some commemorative tribute? Where is it taking place, Ireland, Pennsylvania, or eastern Europe? Why the rugs? Why the flower pots?

If we take the print apart, three figures dominate the scene: a girl in a barrow, a man patting the head of ayoungster, and an old woman with flowers. What are they doing and what is their relationship to the rugs? The old woman is placing flowerpots on the borders of rugs. Why? Is this a ritual? The girl is sickly. Where is she being taken? What of the man patting the youngster's head? Is he a central figure or merely centrally figured? And why is the sickly girl being rolled toward the river while everyone else is coming from it?

This is a rug Rorschach! Everyone who has seen this print has a different story. What's yours?

Carpets In Unexpected Space

36. Mystery print from 1893.

Carpet Diem!

37. Here, they park the carpets!

Kilimologists carefully study rugs, believing every carpet has a story to tell in symbol, color, and design. They seek to translate the stories hidden amidst floral motifs and geometric schemes. Rugs also have their histories, magical and mundane, which arise from use. And rug dealers cherish both. Like *Scheherazade*, there are 1001 carpet tales.

Old Baghdad had its travelling carpets, but they're hard to find these days. A customer purchased a fine Persian rug for her luxury auto. She chose a *pushti*, a little rug measuring two by three feet, which she fondly named her "Car-Pet." A rug to ride on!

All well and good, but what about the woman in the picture? Here is a nightmare in the making for a rug professional. What painful butchery must these "Car-Pets" endure to conform to the confines of an auto? A travesty in truncation!

Any kind of rug reduction is painful to a carpet dealer. A woeful tale is told of an antique *Mohtashem*, a fine quality carpet woven in Kashan, returned for removal of inner borders. For a carpet guardian, this request exceeded the permissible. The dealer refused. He protested he could not violate the rug. Sorrowfully, the customer found someone who would!

The Moral of our tales: Fit the room to the rug, not the rug to the room!

Carpet Diem!

Oriental rugs can be an indispensable accent to our personal, professional, and playful lives. We grow up and grow old upon them. Carpets share our moments of joyous celebration, vocational triumph, and tender sorrow, all the experiences that have made us who we are. Some are born upon a carpet, some marry upon them, and others die with them.

Whether your rug is an instrument of authority, a display of grandeur, a cherished heirloom, a sacred companion, an exotic accessory, or a place of whimsy, it will serve you well. Your rug may contain natural, geometric, or abstract designs in hues wild or subtle. It may show the rough hand of a nomadic tribesman or the splendid precision of a master weaver. But that rug of yours is more than material, dyes, and workmanship. It is a creation born of imagination and skill, a magnificent possession.

A treasure to treasure for a lifetime.

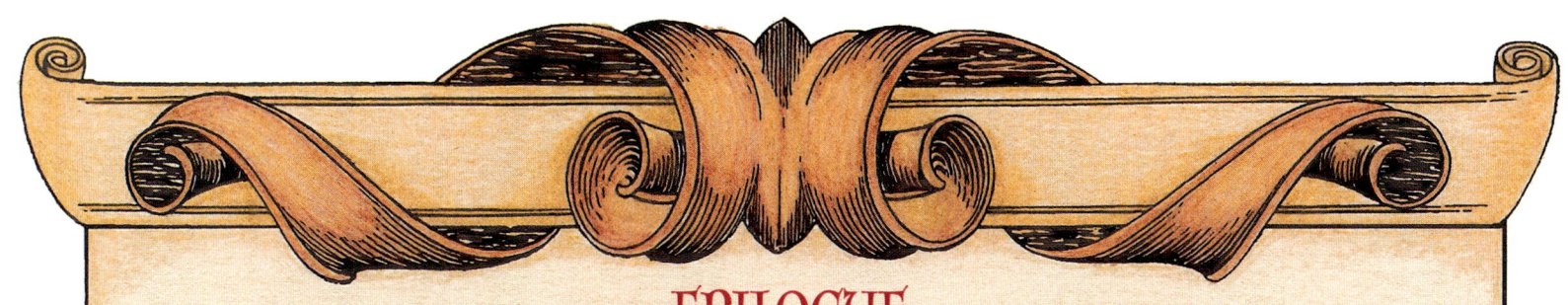

EPILOGUE

Once Upon A Carpet
walk barefoot, sole to soul.
Amazing!
There is something in that soft texture,
searching
to connect with you.
Open your irises,
let the carpet's reflected light re-form in your mind.
Here is a composition only you, with your carpet,
can create.
Walk to the fringe,
turn around,
penetrate the pattern.
There is a message,
the song of your carpet that only you will ever hear.
This is your carpet connection.

In the carpet continuum
you are the essential link.
Your carpet carries the tales, the poetry, and the vision
from generations unremembered.
This tulip, that rose, these arrows,
this gold, that crimson,
this pattern, that tattered fringe.
You are the passage,
making a creative collaboration
reaching back farther than memory,
extending to unknowable future.
Within you
the epic which is your carpet
mingles
with the history that is your life.
Bearing fruit,
        a legacy which endures, ever
                . . . after.

Morning overtakes me, and like Scheherazade, I lapse into silence.

Kathleen Ryniker Bashian

ENDNOTES

Chapter I: If These Rugs Could Talk! Carpets in Diplomatic Space

Page 9

Rugs and carpets are the same things; but carpets are bigger. These terms will be used interchangeably throughout the text.

Page 10

The range of connotations for the term, *carpet knight*, swings between disparaging "dilettante" who spends time in idleness and pleasure and a "stay at home soldier," one who serves on other battlefields on a carpet. In the context of the *Somerset House Conference* painting, among those commissioned as members of the negotiating delegation some would have been *carpet knights*.

In the group portrait of this *Somerset House Conference* the delegation representing Spain and the Catholic Netherlands is on the left from the window: Juan de Valasco, Duke of Frias, Constable of Castile; Juan de Tasis, Count of Villa Mediana; Alessandro Robida, Senator of Milan; Charles de Ligne, Count of Aremberg; Jean Richardot, President of the Privy Council; Louis Vereyken, Audencier of Brussels. On the right are the English delegates: Thomas Sackville, Earl of Dorset; Charles Howard, Earl of Nottingham; Charles Blount, Earl of Devonshire; Henry Howard, Earl of Northampton; Robert Cecil, Viscount Cranborne.

Carpets are evident on tables in historical portraits and genre paintings of Dutch, English, French, and Italian artists well into the eighteenth century. Dr. Johnson's *Dictionary* (1822 edition) defines carpet as "any covering made of thick material especially a table cover," p. 264.

Page 12

Almost every participant of the Yalta Conference has written about this historic encounter, perhaps the most famous of the Allied meetings during WWII. This account was taken from Joseph Alsop, *FDR: A Centenary Remembrance, 1882-1945* (New York: Pocket Books, 1982), p. 229.

Page 14

I am grateful to Jack Green of the Curator Branch of the Naval Historical Foundation in Washington, DC, for locating and providing this photograph and the story behind the meeting aboard the *Quincy*. FDR's plane, the *Sacred Cow*, can now be seen at Wright-Patterson AFB.

Information about FDR's gifts to the Saudi ruler, a wheelchair and penicillin, was also taken from Alsop's book, *FDR's Last Year*.

Page 16

I am grateful to the docents of Vizcaya for information about the carpet prohibition during this state meeting between President Reagan and Pope John Paul II.

Page 17

The full text of Franklin's missive is found in the *Papers of Benjamin Franklin*, ed. Leonard Labaree (New Haven: Yale University Press, 1969), vol. 12, January 1765-December 1765, p. 297. Although Franklin's letter to Deborah was written in October 1765, she did not receive it until April 1766. I calculate the value of a 10-guinea purchase in 1766 to be $55.

Page 18

Grateful thanks to Robert Melhorn and Cheryl Ryefield of the Office of Public Affairs of the Department of the Army in Washington, DC, for locating and providing this photograph of General Schwarzkopf meeting with now Emir Hamad bin Isa al-Khalifa of Bahrain. For further information pertaining to this meeting see General Khaled bin Sultan, *Desert Warrior* (New York: Harper Collins, 1995).

Page 19

Grateful thanks to Jennifer Loynd, Art Collection Manager, Foreign building Operation, for information about the Diplomatic Reception Rooms of the United States Department of State. Tours are available by reservation, sure to delight any carpet lover.

Chapter II: Roll Out the Red Carpet! Carpets in Privileged Space

Page 22

Palace carpet is the name given to any carpet bigger than 14ft x 24ft. These were created specifically for regal adornment, or to be given as diplomatic gifts throughout the world. Shah Abbas I of the Safavid dynasty (1586-1628) institutionalized this tradition when he instructed his court weavers, "Make me a carpet to mirror my magnificence!" (Reported by English traveler, Thomas Herbert, Travels in Persia, 1627-1629, ed. Sir Wm. Foster [New York: Books for Libraries Press, 1929], p. 13).

Royal carpet workshops were established by: Mughal Emperor Akbar the Great (1542-1605). French King Henry IV (1553-1610) began ateliers (factory workshops in France) and his successor Louis XIII (1601-1643) established the Savonnerie factories.

Henry VIII is one of the first English monarchs to import oriental rugs. Part of the inventory of the Wardrobe and Household stuff of King Henry VIII, made by commission dated 14 September 1547, is available at the British Museum, Harl. MS, 1419B. Henry's carpet collection at Windsor Castle is itemized in *HALI* (1981), vol. 3, no. 3.

Readers interested in a more complete explanation of Renaissance fashion and its meaning might consult the works of Anne Hollander, in particular, *Seeing Through Clothes, or Sex and Suits* (New York: Alfred Knopf, 1994). Though this portrait of Henry VIII is perhaps the best known, there are at least seven other regal carpet portraits.

Page 25

Richard McLanathan, *Gilbert Stuart* (New York: Harry Abrams, 1986) provides illustrations of other portraits of George Washington, in particular, one which now hangs in the New York Public Library. This portrait is of interest to the rug enthusiast for one picture has a rug, the other none. The photograph without the rug lacks impact and one can readily understand why the carpeted portrait is a national icon.

Washington's letter to James Madison was written from Mount Vernon on March 30, 1789. See *Writings of Washington,* 1745-1799, ed. John Fitzpatrick (Washington, DC: Government Printing Office, 1939), vol. 30, p. 255.

Page 27

For further information about the fascinating kingdom of Bhutan consult: *Bhutan Mountain Fortress of the Gods,* general eds. Christian Schicklgruber and Francoise Pommaret (Boston: Shambhala, 1998) or Barbara Crossette, *So Close To Heaven: The Vanishing Buddhist Kingdoms of the Himalayas* (New York: Random House, 1995).

Page 28

The colloquial expression, "On the carpet," was coined in the early 19th century. Charles Earle Funk, *Heavens to Betsy! And Other Curious Sayings* (New York: Harper and Row, 1955), p. 62.

Page 29

Caroline Bosly, *Rugs to Riches* (New York: Pantheon, 1980), p. 7, refers to Persian King Chosroes I (531-579 AD). To celebrate his defeat of the Romans and his conquest of southern Arabia, Chosroes ordered this special *Spring Carpet* which weighed more than two tons and measured 400ft x 100ft! It is believed to be the most expensive carpet ever made! King Chosroes could stroll down its woven paths and stand beside its woven flowerbeds.

Page 30

There is some controversy about the identification of this rug. Experts I have consulted uniformly claim the rug on Freud's couch is a *Shiraz* rug, one of the tribes of the Qashqai confederacy. Freud's brother-in-law was a rug importer who may well have provided the inveterate collector Freud with his carpets.

Page 32

Generations have been fascinated with the Gilded Age, the arrival of the merchant class in America. Cleveland Amory, *The Last Resorts: Newport in its Glory 1890-1914* (New York: Harper, 1952) takes special delight in enumerating anecdotes about the rich and their rugs (the Fairman Rogers' story, p. 176; and the story of Mrs. Astor, p. 189.)

Chapter III: From Cradle to Grave! Carpets in Domestic Space

Page 36

While researching this book I interviewed many people with carpet memories from childhood, many adult carpet owners with children, and people whose family histories include carpet tales. I have selected some of the fondest of these stories which I hope will register with you. Grateful thanks to Patricia Zakian Tith and Robert McMillan for sharing their stories.

Page 41

The engagement of Nicholas and Alexandra took place on the wedding day of Alix's brother Ernie to Saxe-Coburg Princess Victoria Melita, another grand daughter of Queen Victoria. Though Emperor Wilhelm II, Queen Victoria, and innumerable European royalty were assembled in Coburg for this event, the spotlight was clearly upon Nicholas and Alix. For more information, see Edvard Radzinsky, *The Last Tsar: The Life and Death of Nicholas II,* trans. Marian Schwartz (New York: Doubleday, 1992), p. 34.

Page 43

The terms dowry, marriage, and wedding rugs have specific meanings but are often used interchangeably. Marriage rugs can be made by the principals or given to the principals on their wedding day. For further information pertaining to dowry rugs consult Roger Cavanna of the Carpets of the Inner Circle gallery in San Francisco who recently hosted an exhibition of dowry weavings. Caroline Bosly, op. cit., p. 71 notes that in a marriage tree rug, when a main branch is sawn off this means it is a second marriage for one of the partners.

Page 44

Let me brave the minefield of rug reading. All of us are aware of at least two camps: those who read rugs literally and those who see no meaning beyond a pretty design. Symbols found in domestic rugs, those relating to betrothal, marriage, pregnancy, birth and death, are often the source of most intense debate. The discussion is vital and illuminating and I intend to pursue it in the future.

Page 47

It is hard to overstate the importance of hospitality in Eastern culture. The obligatory hospitality of a hearth rug is inviolable. See A. Cecil Edwards, *The Persian Carpet* (London, 1953) for a description of hearth rugs.

Chapter IV: This is Holy Ground! Carpets in Sacred Space

Page 50

I am grateful to the information office of the Saudi Arabian embassy in Washington, DC, for explanation of *salat* and its relationship to prayer rugs.

Mosque rugs are a mixture of votive donations in thanksgiving, in commemoration, in tribute, as well as those given in memoriam of a loved one. For further information about rugs in a Turkish mosque see Henry Glassie, *Turkish Traditional Art Today* (Bloomington: Indiana University Press, 1993), p. 594.

Page 52

Prayer rugs are sacrosanct. In 1610, the highest Ottoman religious authority ruled against the use of religious symbols (e.g. mihrab, words of the Koran, etc.) in carpets for export. The prohibition against walking upon holy symbols could not be controlled outside Moslem countries. For

Endnotes

further information see Rosamond E. Mack, "Lotto: A Carpet Connoisseur," *Lorenzo Lotto*, ed. David Alan Brown, Peter Humfrey and Mauro Lucco (Washington: National Gallery of Art, 1997), pp. 59-67.

Page 53

Grateful thanks to Grazia Tozzi for assistance in securing the rights to reproduce the painting, *Evening Prayer*.

Page 55

Such a good book! Anton Felton, *Jewish Carpets: A History and Guide* (England: Antique Collectors Club, 1997). Like most of you, I was only marginally aware of Jewish carpet traditions. This book provides convincing scholastic investigation into a field worthy of further attention.

Page 56

Paul Geers, a rug dealer from St. Louis, MO, informs me that when Pope John Paul II performed mass there, rugs were requested on loan for the occasion. It appears that the carpet tradition seen in the Gdansk photograph continues.

Page 59

There is nothing to match the splendor of viewing rugs within a cathedral glowing with late afternoon light.

Chapter V: Oriental Mystique! Carpets in Exotic Space

Page 62

Orientalism is a term loosely used to define characteristics of things Eastern adopted into Western subjects. Orientalism is often used to describe Western painting, poetry, and music inspired by an oriental subject.

Accounts of Cleopatra rendered to Caesar in an oriental rug are legendary, and every major film version of *Cleopatra* includes this episode as a moment of high drama. The rugs are every bit as beautiful as the women in them, e.g., Claudette Colbert (1934), Vivian Leigh (1946) and Elizabeth Taylor (1963).

Page 64

Homer's account of the Circe story can be found in *The Odyssey*, trans. E. V. Rieu (Penguin Books, 1991), 4.120-35.

Page 65

Contemporary artist Claudio Bravo (b.1936) frequently features oriental rugs beautifully rendered such as we see in this *Circe* painting.

Page 69

For a vivid account of Gertrude Vanderbilt Whitney's activities in Paris see Clarice Stasz, *The Vanderbilt Women: Dynasty of Wealth, Glamour and Tragedy* (New York: St. Martin's Press, 1991).

For utterly delightful, lush illustrations of the costume design of Leon Bakst see *The Decorative Art of Leon Bakst*, trans. Harry Melvill (New York: Dover Publications, 1972).

Page 71

Since carpets are a major export product of Morocco, you may find a government stamp of approval on the backside of the carpet. These carpets, woven in the bright sunlight of the Middle East, take on a different hue when placed in the more temperate zones of Europe and North America.

Page 72

See Henry Glassie, op. cit., *Turkish Traditional Art Today*, for a discussion of the Turkish delight in the color red.

Chapter VI: Carpet Diem! Carpets in Unexpected Space

Page 76

Many a family has told the story of their elders who in the 1940's threw away "old" oriental rugs for they were deemed old fashioned! Happily, this story is not often repeated with the current generations who appreciate the value of antique oriental rugs.

Page 77

Among the many tales I have heard about cleaning rugs in water, I enjoy Caroline Bosly's report, op. cit., p.144, that after a snowfall Scandinavians will put a rug in a garage to chill overnight. The next morning, the rug is placed, face down, on the fresh snow and gently beaten with twigs to loosen dirt. As long as the rug remains cold, it will not get soggy. This is the ultimate natural clean!

Page 79

Christie's could not identify the purchaser of the *Seeteppich*, but I hope to eventually speak with the new owner.

Page 81

This sand carpet at the beach is just one of the many unusual places in which oriental carpets can be found. Other carpet sightings include ceilings, stables, floats and boats.

Page 85

This carpet conundrum print has provoked lengthy discussion and curious speculation. Most viewers concur that what we see represents real rugs, not sand paintings.

Page 87

There surely are other uses for Car-Pets taken on the road! May you find joy discovering them!

SELECT BIBLIOGRAPHY

Allane, Lee. *Oriental Rugs A Buyer's Guide.* London: Thames and Hudson, 1997.

Aschenbrenner, Eric. *Persian Rugs and Carpets.* Iran: Farhang-Sara, 1994.

Bosly, Caroline. *Rugs to Riches: An Insider's Guide to Buying Oriental Rugs.* New York: Pantheon Books, 1980.

Calatchi, Robert de. *Oriental Carpets.* London: Alpine Fine Arts Collection, 1994.

Denny, Walter. *Southeby's Guide to Oriental Carpets.* New York: Fireside Books, 1994.

Eastern Carpets in the Western World: From the 15th to the 17th Century, ed. Donald King and David Sylvester. London: Arts Council of Britain, 1983.

Edwards, A. Cecil. *The Persian Carpet A Survey of the Carpet-Weaving Industry of Persia.* London: Gerald Duckworth and Co. LTD, 1960.

Ellwanger, W. D. *The Oriental Rug.* Dodd, Mead & Co., 1906.

Erdmann, K. *700 Years of Oriental Carpets.* London: 1970.

Felton, Anton. *Jewish Carpets: A History and Guide.* England: Antique Collectors' Club, 1997.

Formenton, Fabio. *Oriental Rugs and Carpets.* New York: McGraw Hill, 1972.

Gantzhorn, Volkmar. *Oriental Carpets: Their Iconology and Iconography from Earliest Times to the 18th Century.* Germany: Taschen, 1998.

Glassie, Henry. Turkish Traditional Art Today. Bloomington: Indiana University Press, 1993.

Great Carpets of the World, ed. Susan Day. London: Thames and Hudson, 1996.

Gregorian, Arthur. *Oriental Rugs and the Stories They Tell.* Boston: Nimrod Press, 1967.

Middleton, Andrew. *Rugs and Carpets: Techniques, Traditions & Designs.* London: Mitchell Beazley, 1996.

Mills, John. "Carpets in Paintings." *HALI* #13. August 1991.

Noonan, James-Charles. *The Church Visible: The Ceremonial Life and Protocol of the Roman Catholic Church.* New York: Viking, 1996.

Stone, Peter. *The Oriental Rug Lexicon.* Seattle: University of Washington Press, 1997.

Summers-Herbert, Janice. *Oriental Rugs: The Illustrated Guide.* New York: MacMillan, 1982.

The Arabian Nights. trans. Husain Haddawy. New York: Norton and Company, 1990.

Thompson, John. *Oriental Carpets: From the Tents, Cottages and Workshops of Asia.* Dutton Studio Books, 1993.

Walker, Daniel. *Flowers Underfoot: Indian Carpets of the Mughal Era.* New York: Metropolitan Museum of Art, 1997.

PICTURE CREDITS

1. (Cover and frontispiece) Pirniakan Antique Collection, Newport Beach, CA.
2. Bashian Bros., Inc., Secaucus, NJ.
3. National Portrait Gallery, London.
4. Imperial War Museum, London.
5. Naval Historical Foundation, Washington, DC.
6. S.Sgt. Dean Wagner/Office of Public Affairs, Department of the Army, Washington, DC.
7. Bashian Bros., Inc., Secaucus, NJ.
8. Belvoir Castle, Duke of Rutland Collection, Leicestershire, England.
9. White House Collection, copyright White House Historical Association.
10. James Stanfield/National Geographic Society Image Collection.
11. Nick Bagguley/Freud Museum Collection, London.
12. Bashian Bros., Inc., Secaucus, NJ.
13. Doris Leslie Blau, New York, NY.
14. Central State Archive of Film and Photographic Documents of the U.S.S.R.
15. Turkish Republic, *Turkish Handwoven Carpets*, Catalogue No. 1, 1988.
16. Turkish Republic, *Turkish Handwoven Carpets*, Catalogue No. 1, 1988.
17. Photofest, New York, NY.
18. Bashian Bros., Inc., Secaucus, NJ.
19. James Stanfield/National Geographic Society Image Collection.
20. Museo di Capodimonte, Naples, Italy.
21. The Textile Museum, Washington, D.C., no. R16.4.4. Acquired by George Hewitt Myers in 1915.
22. James Stanfield/National Geographic Society Image Collection.
23. James Stanfield/National Geographic Society Image Collection.
24. Bashian Bros., Inc., Secaucus, NJ.
25. Photofest, New York, NY.
26. Marlborough Gallery, New York, NY.
27. Photofest, New York, NY.
28. Flora Biddle, the Gertrude Vanderbilt Whitney Papers.
29. James Stanfield/National Geographic Society Image Collection.
30. Berko Fine Paintings, Knokke-Heist.
31. Bashian Bros., Inc., Secaucus, NJ.
32. Haji Mohamed Khan Zephyr Amir, *The World of Supreme Persian Carpets*, Iran.
33. Christie's Images, Ltd., 1999.
34. Central State Archive and Photographic Documents of the U.S.S.R.
35. Paramount.
36. Mystery print of 1893 by? Gebbie and Company.
37. Haji Mohamed Khan Zephyr Amir, *The World of Supreme Persian Carpets*, Iran.

Kathleen Ryniker Bashian is no stranger to oriental rugs having married into a family whose business, and passion, is rugs. She is the founder of *Cultural Connections*™, a business which develops programs to showcase the history and mystery of products and services in the company of the classics. *Cultural Connections*™ reveals the connection between a product/service and culture, through history, poetry, drama, painting, and music.

Dr. Bashian is a professional speaker and a member of the National Speakers Association. A popular speaker at association conventions, motivational marketing seminars, and gala retail events, her multi-disciplinary presentations have received strong audience acclaim and media endorsement.

Dr. Bashian is a university scholar in the arts and humanities who holds a B.A. from Brooklyn College, and a M.A. and Ph.D. from New York University, with specialization in Shakespeare. She has taught at George Washington University, Marymount University, and George Mason University in Virginia. Her work has been recognized by grants from the National Endowment for the Humanities.

The author lives in McLean, Virginia with her husband and three children. Readers are welcome to visit her website to learn more about *Cultural Connections*™, to order copies of her book, and to share special rug stories.

http://www.CULTURALCON.COM